Keys to a
Healthy MARRIAGE
By Damion Williams

Table of Contents

Keys to a Healthy Marriage
Introduction

Marriage is a beautiful and rewarding experience, but it is not without its challenges. As couples navigate the ups and downs of life together, conflicts and misunderstandings can arise, leading to feelings of frustration, resentment, and loneliness. In times like these, a marriage counselor can provide invaluable support, guidance, and insight.
In this book, we will explore the role of the marriage counselor in helping couples build and sustain a healthy relationship. We will examine the challenges that couples face and the strategies that counselors use to help them overcome these obstacles. From communication skills to conflict resolution techniques, we will provide practical advice and actionable steps that can be used by anyone looking to improve their relationship.

Chapter 1: The Importance of Marriage Counseling
In this chapter, we will discuss why marriage counseling is important and how it can benefit couples. We will explore the common issues that bring couples to counseling and the benefits of seeking professional help. We will also address the common misconceptions about counseling and explain how it can be a positive and transformative experience for couples.

Chapter 2: Understanding Relationship Dynamics
In this chapter, we will explore the dynamics of relationships and how they can impact a couple's ability to communicate and resolve conflicts. We will discuss the importance of emotional intelligence and the role it plays in fostering healthy relationships. We will also examine the different attachment styles that individuals may have and how these can impact their relationships.

Chapter 3: Communication Skills for Healthy Relationships
Effective communication is essential for building and sustaining a healthy relationship. In this chapter, we will provide practical advice and techniques for improving communication between couples. We will explore active listening, effective expression of emotions, and other key communication skills that

can help couples better understand each other and resolve conflicts.

Chapter 4: Conflict Resolution Strategies

All relationships will face conflict at some point. In this chapter, we will examine the common sources of conflict in relationships and provide strategies for resolving conflicts in a healthy and productive manner. We will also explore the importance of forgiveness and how it can help couples move past difficult experiences.

Chapter 5: Building and Maintaining Intimacy

Intimacy is a vital component of any healthy relationship. In this chapter, we will explore the different types of intimacy and provide strategies for building and maintaining intimacy over the course of a long-term relationship. We will also discuss the common barriers to intimacy and how to overcome them.

Chapter 6: Strengthening the Marriage Bond

In this chapter, we will examine the importance of strengthening the bond between partners. We will explore the different ways that couples can build and maintain a strong connection, including shared experiences, gratitude, and other positive habits. We will also discuss the role of commitment in a healthy relationship.

Marriage counseling can be a transformative experience for couples looking to improve their relationship. By providing support, guidance, and practical advice, a marriage counselor can help couples navigate the challenges of married life and build a healthy and lasting bond. By using the strategies outlined in this book, couples can improve their communication, resolve conflicts, and build a strong and intimate connection.

Wherefore they are no more twain, but One flesh. What therefore God hath joined together, let not man put asunder.

Matthew 19;6 NKJV

Chapter 1
The Importance of Marriage Counseling

Marriage counseling is a type of therapy designed to help couples navigate the challenges of married life and build a strong and healthy relationship. While many couples may feel that they can work through their problems on their own, the reality is that marriage counseling can be an invaluable resource for improving communication, resolving conflicts, and strengthening the bond between partners. There are many reasons why marriage counseling can be important for couples. Some of the key benefits of marriage counseling include:

Improved Communication: Communication is the foundation of any healthy relationship. Marriage counseling can help couples learn how to communicate more effectively, express their needs and feelings, and listen to each other with empathy and understanding.

Conflict Resolution: All couples will face conflicts at some point in their relationship. Marriage counseling can provide couples with tools and strategies for resolving conflicts in a healthy and productive manner, reducing tension and improving the overall quality of the relationship.

Strengthened Intimacy: Intimacy is a key component of any healthy relationship, but it can be difficult to maintain over time. Marriage counseling can help couples improve their emotional and physical intimacy, build trust and closeness, and reignite the spark in their relationship.

Greater Understanding: Marriage counseling can help couples gain a deeper understanding of each other, their values, and their goals. This can help to build a stronger foundation for the relationship and improve overall compatibility.

A Safe Space to Address Issues: Marriage counseling provides a safe and neutral space for couples to address sensitive issues, discuss their concerns, and work through problems without judgment or criticism.

Ultimately, the importance of marriage counseling lies in its ability to help couples build a strong and healthy relationship that can weather the challenges of married life. Whether a couple is struggling with communication issues, trust issues, or simply needs help reigniting their passion for each other, marriage counseling can provide the guidance and support needed to create a more fulfilling and satisfying relationship.

Chapter 2
Understanding Relationship Dynamics

Relationship dynamics refers to the complex interactions and patterns of behavior that occur between two people in a relationship. Understanding relationship dynamics is crucial for maintaining healthy relationships, resolving conflicts, and improving communication between partners. Here are some key factors to consider when analyzing relationship dynamics:

Communication: Effective communication is essential for building healthy relationships. This includes both verbal and non-verbal communication. Communication patterns can vary greatly from one relationship to another and can play a significant role in determining the overall health and stability of the relationship.

Power Dynamics: Power dynamics refers to the balance of power between partners in a relationship. This can include things like decision-making, financial control, and emotional control. When one partner has more power than the other, it can create feelings of resentment, frustration, and powerlessness.

Attachment Styles: Attachment styles are patterns of behavior and thought that develop in childhood and continue into adulthood, influencing how people interact in relationships. There are four main attachment styles: secure, anxious, avoidant, and fearful avoidant. Understanding your own attachment style and your partner's can help you better understand your behavior and interactions within the relationship.

<u>Trust</u>: Trust is the foundation of any healthy relationship. When trust is broken, it can be difficult to repair the relationship. Trust can be eroded by things like lying, betrayal, and infidelity.

<u>Emotional Intimacy</u>: Emotional intimacy is the closeness and connection that develops between two people over time. It involves sharing thoughts, feelings, and experiences with your partner in a safe and supportive environment. Emotional intimacy is crucial for building a strong and healthy relationship.

Commitment in marriage refers to the dedication and loyalty that partners have towards each other. It involves a deep sense of responsibility, faithfulness, and dedication to the relationship.

Commitment in marriage means that both partners are willing to work through challenges and difficulties together, and that they prioritize the well-being of the relationship above their individual needs or desires. It involves making a conscious decision to remain faithful and supportive to one's spouse, even during times of conflict or hardship.

To cultivate commitment in marriage, it's important to prioritize communication and trust in the relationship. This means actively listening to your partner's concerns and needs, expressing your own in a respectful way, and being honest and transparent with each other.

Other important aspects of commitment in marriage include making time for each other, supporting each other's goals and aspirations, and being willing to compromise and make sacrifices when necessary. It's also important to be willing to seek help from a therapist or counselor if needed, in order to work through any challenges or issues in the relationship.

Overall, commitment in marriage is a crucial aspect of a strong and healthy partnership. By prioritizing dedication, loyalty, and trust in the relationship, partners can build a foundation of mutual respect and support that can withstand the tests of time and challenges that arise in life.

Devotion in marriage refers to a strong commitment and loyalty to one's spouse. It involves a deep sense of dedication, sacrifice, and love for one's partner, even in the face of challenges and difficulties. Devotion in marriage means putting your partner's needs and interests ahead of your own. It involves being supportive, understanding, and patient with your spouse, and working together to overcome any obstacles that come your way.

To cultivate devotion in marriage, it's important to prioritize communication and intimacy with your partner. This means actively listening to their thoughts and feelings, expressing your own in a respectful way, and making time for quality time together.

Other important aspects of devotion in marriage include honesty, trust, and forgiveness. It's essential to be open and honest with your spouse about your thoughts, feelings, and actions, and to trust that they will do the same. Forgiveness is also key, as it allows you to move past any mistakes or hurts and continue to build a strong, loving relationship.

Overall, devotion in marriage is a crucial aspect of a successful and fulfilling partnership. By prioritizing your commitment to your spouse and working together to build a strong foundation of trust, communication, and love, you can create a long-lasting and meaningful relationship.

Conflict Resolution: All relationships experience conflicts from time to time. The way couples handle conflicts can have a significant impact on the overall health and stability of the relationship. Effective conflict resolution involves active listening, empathizing with your partner's perspective, and finding mutually agreeable solutions.

In summary, understanding relationship dynamics involves examining communication patterns, power dynamics, attachment styles, trust, emotional intimacy, commitment and devotion and conflict resolution. By understanding these factors, couples can identify areas of strength and weakness in their relationship and work to build a stronger and healthier connection.

Chapter 3
Communication Skills for Healthy Relationships

Effective communication is a crucial component of healthy relationships. It involves expressing yourself clearly and actively listening to your partner's needs and concerns. Here are some communication skills that can help improve the quality of your relationships:

<u>Active Listening</u>: Active listening involves paying attention to what your partner is saying, asking questions to clarify their perspective, and paraphrasing what they've said to show that you understand. This helps your partner feel heard and valued.

<u>Using "I" Statements</u>: "I" statements focus on your own feelings and needs, rather than placing blame

or making accusations. For example, instead of saying "You never listen to me," you might say "I feel unheard when I try to share my thoughts with you."

<u>Avoiding Defensiveness</u>: When we feel attacked or criticized, our instinct may be to become defensive. However, defensiveness can escalate conflicts and prevent effective communication. Try to remain calm and open to your partner's perspective.

<u>Using Non-Verbal Communication</u>: Non-verbal cues like facial expressions, tone of voice, and body language can convey a lot of information in a conversation. Pay attention to your own non-verbal cues and try to interpret your partner's as well.

<u>Taking Breaks</u>: If a conversation becomes heated or emotionally charged, it can be helpful to take a break and come back to it later when both parties have had time to cool down and reflect.

<u>Using Assertive Communication</u>: Assertive communication involves expressing your needs and boundaries in a clear and direct manner, while still being respectful of your partner's needs and feelings. This can help prevent misunderstandings and build trust.

<u>Showing Empathy</u>: Empathy involves putting yourself in your partner's shoes and trying to understand their perspective. This can help create a sense of connection and promote healthy communication.

In summary, effective communication is essential for healthy relationships. By practicing active listening, using "I" statements, avoiding defensiveness, using non-verbal communication, taking breaks, using assertive communication, and showing empathy, you can improve the quality of your communication with your partner and build a stronger and healthier relationship.

Chapter 4
Conflict Resolution Strategies

Conflicts are a normal part of any relationship, but how you handle them can make a big difference in the health and longevity of your relationship. Here are some effective conflict resolution strategies:

<u>Take a Break</u>: If emotions are running high, it can be helpful to take a break and come back to the conversation when you're both feeling calmer.

<u>Use "I" Statements</u>: "I" statements help you take responsibility for your own feelings and avoid blaming or attacking your partner. For example, instead of saying "You're always so selfish," you might say "I feel hurt when you don't take my needs into account."

<u>Listen Actively</u>: Listening actively involves paying attention to what your partner is saying, asking

clarifying questions, and summarizing what you've heard to show that you understand.

<u>Use Humor</u>: Using humor can help defuse tension and lighten the mood during a conflict. Just make sure the humor isn't at your partner's expense.

<u>Find Common Ground</u>: Try to find areas where you both agree and build from there. This can help create a sense of unity and make it easier to work through disagreements.

<u>Practice Empathy</u>: Empathy involves putting yourself in your partner's shoes and trying to understand their perspective. This can help you see the conflict from their point of view and find common ground.

<u>Brainstorm Solutions</u>: Work together to come up with solutions that address both of your needs. Be open to compromise and creative problem-solving.

<u>Apologize</u>: If you've done something wrong, apologize sincerely and make amends.

<u>Seek Help</u>: If you're struggling to resolve conflicts on your own, consider seeking the help of a therapist or counselor.

Holding one accountable in marriage means being responsible for your actions and accepting the consequences of your decisions. It involves taking ownership of your behavior and being willing to acknowledge when you have made mistakes or hurt your partner.

When partners hold each other accountable in marriage, they set clear expectations and boundaries for each other, and they hold themselves and each other to those standards. This helps to build trust and respect in the relationship, and it allows partners to address issues or concerns before they become bigger problems.

To hold one accountable in marriage, it's important to communicate openly and honestly with each other. This means expressing your feelings and concerns in a respectful way and being willing to listen to your partner's perspective as well.

It's also important to establish clear expectations and boundaries for each other, and to hold each other to those standards. This means being willing to have difficult conversations when necessary and being open to feedback and constructive criticism from your partner.

In order to hold one accountable in marriage, it's important to approach the situation with empathy and understanding. It's important to recognize that everyone makes mistakes, and that holding each other accountable is about helping each other grow and improve, rather than criticizing or blaming each other.

Overall, holding one accountable in marriage is an important aspect of building a strong and healthy partnership. By communicating openly and honestly, setting clear expectations and boundaries, and approaching the situation with empathy and understanding, partners can work together to build a foundation of trust and respect that can withstand the tests of time and challenges that arise in life.

In summary, conflicts are a normal part of relationships, but how you handle them can make all the difference. By taking a break, using "I" statements, listening actively, using humor, finding common ground, practicing empathy, brainstorming solutions, apologizing, holding one accountable and seeking help when needed, you can improve your conflict resolution skills and build stronger, healthier relationships.

Chapter 5
Building and Maintaining Intimacy

Intimacy is an essential component of any healthy relationship. It involves emotional, physical, and spiritual closeness and can help deepen your connection with your partner. Here are some strategies for building and maintaining intimacy:
Prioritize Quality Time: Make time to be together without distractions. This can include date nights, weekend getaways, or simply spending time together at home.

Communicate Openly and Honestly: Communication is essential for building intimacy. Be open and honest about your feelings, needs, and desires.
Practice Active Listening: Listen to your partner with an open mind and try to understand their perspective. Ask questions and show that you value their opinions and experiences.
Share Vulnerabilities: Being vulnerable with your partner can help deepen your connection. Share your fears, hopes, and dreams, and allow your partner to do the same.
Be Affectionate: Physical touch can help build intimacy. Hold hands, hug, kiss, and cuddle regularly.
Keep the Romance Alive: Make an effort to keep the romance alive in your relationship. Surprise your partner with thoughtful gestures, write love notes, and express your affection regularly.
Experiment with Sexual Intimacy: Sexual intimacy is an important part of many romantic relationships. Experiment with new techniques or positions, communicate your desires and boundaries, and make an effort to prioritize sexual intimacy.
Take Care of Yourself: Taking care of yourself physically, emotionally, and mentally can help you be a better partner and build intimacy in your relationship.

Practice Forgiveness: No relationship is perfect, and conflicts are inevitable. Practice forgiveness and work through conflicts together, rather than holding grudges or dwelling on past mistakes.

In summary, building and maintaining intimacy in a relationship takes effort and intentionality. Prioritize quality time, communicate openly and honestly, practice active listening, share vulnerabilities, be affectionate, keep the romance alive, experiment with sexual intimacy, take care of yourself, and practice forgiveness. By doing so, you can deepen your connection with your partner and build a stronger, healthier relationship.

Chapter 6
Strengthening the Marriage Bond

Strengthening the marriage bond is an ongoing process that involves a combination of commitment, communication, and effort. Here are some strategies for strengthening the marriage bond:

Prioritize Time Together: Make time for each other regularly, even if it's just a few minutes each day. This can involve sharing a meal, taking a walk, or simply talking about your day.

Communicate Effectively: Communication is key to a strong marriage. Listen actively, express your thoughts and feelings, and be open to feedback from your partner.

<u>Show Appreciation and Gratitude</u>: Make an effort to express appreciation and gratitude for your partner regularly. This can include saying thank you, acknowledging their efforts, and telling them what you love about them.

<u>Be Supportive</u>: Support your partner's goals and dreams and be there for them during challenging times. This can involve offering emotional support, practical help, or simply being a listening ear.

<u>Practice Empathy</u>: Put yourself in your partner's shoes and try to understand their perspective. This can help you avoid misunderstandings and strengthen your connection.

<u>Cultivate Shared Interests</u>: Find activities or hobbies that you enjoy doing together. This can help you bond and create shared memories.

<u>Manage Conflict Effectively</u>: Conflicts are inevitable in any marriage, but how you handle them can make all the difference. Practice active listening, use "I" statements, and be open to compromise.

<u>Seek Help When Needed</u>: If you're struggling with your marriage, don't hesitate to seek the help of a therapist or counselor. They can offer tools and strategies for strengthening your bond and improving communication.

<u>Celebrate Milestones</u>: Celebrate milestones in your marriage, such as anniversaries or significant achievements. This can help you reflect on your journey together and strengthen your bond.

Trust is a crucial component of a successful marriage. It involves being honest and transparent with your partner, keeping your promises, and having confidence in your partner's reliability and faithfulness.

In a trusting marriage, both partners feel secure and respected, and they are able to communicate openly and effectively with each other. Trust allows couples to rely on each other and to work together to overcome challenges and achieve their goals.

To build trust in a marriage, it is important to establish and maintain open communication, to be truthful and transparent with your partner, and to demonstrate your commitment to the relationship through your actions. It is also important to be forgiving and understanding when mistakes are made, and to work together to address any issues that arise.

Trust takes time to build, and it requires ongoing effort and commitment from both partners. However, a strong foundation of trust can help to strengthen and deepen the bond between two people, creating a strong and lasting marriage.

Honesty is a fundamental aspect of any successful marriage. It involves being truthful and transparent with your partner, and having the courage to share your thoughts, feelings, and concerns with them. Honesty is important because it builds trust and fosters a deeper level of intimacy between partners. It allows both individuals to be vulnerable with each other, and to feel safe in sharing their innermost thoughts and emotions.

In a marriage, honesty means being truthful about your actions, thoughts, and feelings, even when it may be difficult or uncomfortable. It means not hiding important information from your partner or keeping secrets, as this can erode trust and damage the relationship.

However, honesty should always be balanced with kindness and empathy. It is important to be honest in a way that is respectful and considerate of your partner's feelings, and to avoid being hurtful or critical.

Couples who prioritize honesty in their marriage tend to have stronger and more resilient relationships. They are better equipped to handle challenges and conflicts and are more likely to build a deep and lasting bond.

Faithfulness is an essential component of a healthy and successful marriage. It involves being committed to your partner and choosing to remain emotionally and physically loyal to them.

For many couples, faithfulness means being sexually exclusive and refraining from engaging in romantic or sexual relationships with anyone else. However, faithfulness can also involve emotional fidelity, which means being committed to your partner on a deep emotional level and avoiding behaviors that could damage the trust and intimacy in your relationship.

Being faithful requires ongoing effort and commitment from both partners. It means being honest and transparent with your partner, and working together to address any issues or concerns that arise in your relationship.

It's important to note that faithfulness is not just about avoiding infidelity, but also about actively nurturing and investing in your relationship. This means spending quality time together, being attentive to your partner's needs, and showing appreciation and affection for each other.

Couples who prioritize faithfulness in their marriage tend to have stronger and more resilient relationships. They are better equipped to navigate challenges and conflicts and are more likely to build a deep and lasting bond based on trust, respect, and mutual support.

God can play an important role in marriage for those who are religious or spiritual. For many couples, faith can provide a strong foundation for their relationship, helping them to navigate challenges and find meaning and purpose in their life together.

For religious couples, having God as a central focus in their marriage can provide a sense of shared values and beliefs. This can help to deepen their sense of connection and commitment to each other and provide a sense of comfort and support during difficult times.

In addition, many couples turn to prayer and spiritual practices to strengthen their relationship and deepen their sense of intimacy. By sharing their spiritual journey with each other, they can grow closer and develop a deeper understanding and appreciation for each other's beliefs and values.

Of course, it's important to remember that everyone's spiritual journey is unique, and there is no one "right" way to integrate faith into a marriage. Couples should communicate openly and honestly with each other about their beliefs and expectations, and work together to find a way to honor their spiritual beliefs in a way that feels authentic and meaningful to both of them.

In summary, strengthening the marriage bond requires commitment, communication, trust, honesty, and effort. Having Faith and trusting in God will also help strengthen your marriage bond tremendously. Prioritize time together, communicate effectively, show appreciation and gratitude, be supportive, practice empathy, cultivate shared interests, manage conflict effectively, seek help when needed, and celebrate milestones. By doing so, you can strengthen your bond and build a long-lasting, fulfilling marriage.

Heartfelt Gratitude for the Support and Love in Our Journey Towards a Healthy Marriage

Dear Kimberly [the love of my life]

I hope this letter finds you enveloped in the warmth and love that you bring into my life every day. Today, as I sit down to express my deepest appreciation, I am overwhelmed with gratitude for the remarkable journey we have shared together. Through thick and thin, you have been my rock, my partner, and my confidante, and for that, I am eternally thankful. I also want to extend my heartfelt thanks to our parents, family, and friends who have played an instrumental role in shaping our lives and supporting our union. Your unwavering love, encouragement, and prayers have meant the world to us. It is through your guidance and wisdom that we have learned invaluable lessons about love, commitment, and perseverance.

In the midst of our journey, we have discovered that marriage is not merely a human institution but a sacred bond that God Himself has ordained. The Bible, the source of timeless wisdom, offers us guidance and encouragement in our pursuit of a healthy and thriving marriage. Allow me to share a few inspiring verses that reflect the profound significance of marriage in the eyes of God:

1. Genesis 2:24: "Therefore a man shall leave his father and his mother and hold fast to his wife, and they shall become one flesh."

This verse reminds us of the divine purpose of marriage — to create a union of two individuals who become one in love, unity, and purpose.

2. Ecclesiastes 4:9-12: "Two are better than one because they have a good return for their labor: If either of them falls down, one can help the other up. But pity anyone who falls and has no one to help them up. Also, if two lie down together, they will keep warm. But how can one keep warm alone? Though one may be overpowered, two can defend themselves. A cord of three strands is not quickly broken."

These verses illustrate the strength and support that comes from the union of two souls. Together, we are stronger, more resilient, and capable of weathering any storm that comes our way.

To my darling Kimberly you are the embodiment of God's grace and love in my life. Your unwavering faith, compassion, and selflessness have been a constant source of inspiration for me. As we continue to navigate the beautiful journey of our marriage, I want you to know that my love for you grows deeper with each passing day. Your presence fills my life with joy, and I am truly blessed to call you, my wife.

To our parents, family, and friends, your unwavering love and support have provided us with a strong foundation on which to build our marriage. Your guidance and encouragement have been invaluable, and we are forever grateful for the role you have played in our lives. In closing, let us remember that a healthy marriage is a lifelong commitment. As we face the joys and challenges that lie ahead, let us rely on the love and strength that God provides, knowing that with His guidance, our union will continue to flourish.

With profound gratitude and endless love, from your loving husband, Damion Williams

www.ingramcontent.com/pod-product-compliance
Lightning Source LLC
Chambersburg PA
CBHW081545250726
48659CB00009B/3085